DR. XAVIER DE SALAS

Francisco José de Goya y Lucientes

BARNES & NOBLE

ART SERIES

BARNES & NOBLE, INC.

NEW YORK

Publishers • Booksellers • Since 1873

Editor: Anthony Bosman
Lay-out: Wim van Stek and Aart Verhoeven
Published in the United States in 1962
by Barnes & Noble, Inc., 105 Fifth Avenue, New York 3, N.Y.
Third printing, 1963
© 1961 and printed in Holland by The Ysel Press Ltd, Deventer

FRANCISCO JOSÉ DE GOYA Y LUCIENTES

In order to understand the scope of Goya's art, his development, and tremendous versatility, it is essential to realize that his work extended over a period of more than sixty years, for he continued to draw and paint until his eighty-second year.

The importance of the time factor is evident when one considers the difference between his attitude towards life in his youth when he happily accepted the world as it was, in his manhood when he began to be critical of it, and in his old age when he became bitterly disillusioned with people and society. Indeed, the world changed completely during his lifetime. The aristocratic society in which he had achieved such a great success disappeared during the Napoleonic wars, and despite the reactionary principles and policies of King Ferdinand, the Spanish society of that day tried to move in the direction of democracy. Long before the end of the eighteenth century Goya was expressing the new ideals in his graphic art and in his paintings.

Goya began his artistic career just at the end of the baroque period. In expressing his thoughts and feelings frankly in his art, as he did, he became the pioneer of new artistic tendencies which were to come to fruition in the nineteenth century.

Two trends dominated the art of his era: classical and romantic. Though these appear to be contradictory, they actually were not. Together they represented a reaction against previous conceptions of art and the search for a new form of expression. For more than fifty years both groups managed to coexist. The classical school, which exalted ideal beauty, placed special emphasis upon drawing, tried to capture movement and to execute drawings in the bas-relief manner, and found great pleasure in single-color pictures. The romantic school, which was less interested in ideal beauty than in individual features, attempted to capture movement in variations of light and color and refused to regard the art of antiquity as their model. Both groups, however, were in full accord in that they strove neither towards the tendencies of the Bolognese school nor towards the decorative graces of the rococo style: they wanted to express absolute truth as they saw it, the classicals by reverting partly to their interpretation of the old, and the romantics through their own creations.

As an artist, Goya was by temperament far removed from the classicals. In a few works he approached classical style, but in the greater part of his work the romantic triumphed.

Francisco Goya was born on March 30, 1746, the son of José Goya and his wife Gracia Lucientes, in the little village of Fuendetodos near Saragossa in the Plains of Aragon. Goya spent his childhood in Saragossa, attended school there, and later found employment in the studio of the mediocre artist José Luzán de Martínez, from whom he learned to draw and, as was customary in studios, copied prints of several masters. At the age of seventeen he went to Madrid and, at the end of 1763, entered a competition for a scholarship at the Royal Academy of San Fernando, but failed, and failed again in 1766. In 1770 he was in Rome, living, if we are to believe his statements of later years, on the proceeds of his art.

Goya's early biographers embroider these and the following years with all kinds of adventures. He is said to have fled from Saragossa to Madrid and to have gone as a toreador to Italy. Soon a legend had grown up around the artist; he was regarded as a striking personality, independent and free of any prejudice, and also as a fearless adventurer and amateur toreador. It may well be that he really did, at one time, stand in the arena, that he was involved in several adventures as well as duels—and no doubt he had many love affairs. But little is actually known of his life during these years.

In Madrid there was much for Goya to see and learn. The kings of the House of Bourbon carried on the policies of the last of the Hapsburgs. Charles II had summoned the great scenic painter Lucas Jordán to carry on his work in Spain; the first of the Bourbon kings, Philip V, brought several French painters into the country—Michel-Ange Houasse, Jean Ranc, and Louis Michel van Loo. They were Goya's immediate predecessors. Goya studied the landscapes and small pictures on manners and morals by Houasse. Van Loo was a good portrait painter whose cabinet pieces show a marked influence upon Goya's later work.

Two of the greatest painters of the day were living in Madrid at the time: Anton Raphael Mengs, the first successful classical painter, and Giovanni Battista Tiepolo. In Tiepolo, the most important artist of the rococo school, the great Venetian school reached its zenith.

While in Italy, Goya no doubt became familiar with the paintings of Domenico Tiepolo, a son of Giovanni Battista, as well as those of Giuseppe Maria Crespi, for one can sense their influence in his later works. As he had also learned fresco painting, on his return from Italy at the end of 1771 he was given the task of preparing several sketches for a mural in the choir vault of the Templo de la Virgen del Pilar at Saragossa. He was also entrusted, in July, 1772, with the execution of a picture with the theme "The Adoration of the Name of the Lord." Among other works which he was commissioned to create in Saragossa at that time are the pictures in the Palace of Sobradiel and the large paintings in the Carthusian monastery Aula Dei. In these works, magnificently conceived and strong in construction, we encounter new characteristics which point in the direction in which he was gradually developing. They are dated from 1773 to 1774, and are probably the last that he did during this period in Saragossa.

In 1775 Goya married Josefa Bayeu, sister of the artists Francisco and Ramón Bayeu, who also came from Aragon and had been instructed in the studio of Luzán. His move to Madrid occurred about this time, perhaps because he had received the first orders for designs for tapestry from A. R. Mengs, the Director of the Royal Weaving Mills. From 1774 to 1792 he continued to work for the mills and did sketches for several tapestries. A theme noticeable throughout his works of this period is that of folk life and rural occupations. He began with hunting and fishing scenes. These subjects—similarly presented by his companions Bayeu, José del Castillo, Aguirre, and others— were of French origin and had already been used in Spain at an earlier date by Houasse and also by Lorenzo Tiepolo, another son of Giovanni Battista. Goya's presentation was initially somewhat clumsy and awkward in construction, but it was not long before he was able to master his task with considerably more skill.

After he had settled in Madrid he began to paint portraits. The oldest-known copy in existence is dated 1774.

During the following years Goya continued to paint designs for tapestries. In 1778 alone, he did some fourteen of these, despite a serious illness. In December he sent samples of his etchings after pictures by Velázquez from the Royal Collection to his boyhood friend Martín Zapater. His studies of the technique of Velázquez provided him with a deep insight into Velázquez's artistic capabilities. Years later, Goya said that Velázquez, Rembrandt, and Nature had been his masters.

In 1780 he was elected a member of the San Fernando Academy. The work he submitted, "The Crucified One," followed the

"Crucifixions" of Mengs and Bayeu. In this painting Goya faithfully followed the academic rules in order to prove that he had mastered the conventional style.

In 1785, when the Academy appointed him as a Deputy Director of the Painting Department, orders began to arrive from the aristocracy; his first patrons were the ducal families of Medinaceli and Osuna. Apart from several portraits of the dukes, he did for them, in 1787, a series of small paintings which were intended for the estate of Alameda near Madrid. Goya painted these in brilliant light colors and with deep feeling. The figures stand out in strong relief. The same *joie de vivre* emanates from these pictures as from the letters to his friend Zapater, in which Goya spoke of how well things were going for him—he was "the happiest man in the world." In June, 1786, Goya was appointed Painter to the King (Charles III). Now he was in a position to have a coach, to select his own clientele, and to invest in shares of the Bank of San Carlos—in short, everything seemed to be going his way.

The magnificent portrait of Francisco Bayeu (now in the Valencia Museum) was painted in this year. The light falling on the dark robe makes the face of his brother-in-law stand out strongly and full of animation. Goya now employed for his tapestries themes similar to those in the genre pictures of the Alameda estate of the Duke of Osuna: "Spring" or "The Flower Girl," "Autumn" or "The Wine Harvest," "Summer" or "The Harvest," "The Injured Bricklayer" (p. 24), "Blind Man's Buff," and later: "Winter," "The Village Wedding," and "The Poor at the Well." With an easy mastery of his medium, he created scenes of great brightness and opacity, charm, and happiness. Some pictures of that period—for example, that of the Marquesa de Pontejos and that of Doña Tadea Arias—are painted in exquisite tones of pale gray, pink, and mauve, almost caressingly applied. Several of Goya's best tapestry designs were created in 1788, notably the "Folk Festival on St. Isidore's Day."

Goya was no landscape artist, and the backgrounds of his pictures reveal how little he was interested in painting landscape, which he apparently regarded as merely a backdrop for human figures. One could associate the "pastoral" or "heroic" landscapes that Goya used for backgrounds with the conventional rules of Piles and the French landscape painters of the Louis XVI period.

The "Folk Festival" was followed by other designs of equal beauty, rich hues, and refreshingly imaginative power: "Blind Man's Buff," "The Little Giant" (p. 20), and "The Stilt-walkers."

An occurrence at the beginning of 1789 effected a change in Goya's life. Charles III died and, on January 17, his son acceded to the throne as Charles IV. On April 25 Goya was appointed Painter to the Court. For the first time he received royal commissions, but he also undertook other work. As far as we know, however, he did not actually paint very much during this year, nor was the following year very productive even though in 1790 he did quite a few portraits in Saragossa and Valencia.

Presumably the striking self-portrait which shows the artist standing at his work was painted in 1790. He is wearing a peculiar hat, the crown of which is encircled by a band bearing miniature candle holders, permitting him to illuminate his subjects without blinding himself. This picture confirms what his son writes: "He paints in one sitting only, which sometimes lasts up to ten hours, but never in the evening; and, in order to heighten the effect of a portrait, he adds the final touches at night under artificial light." This explains several characteristic traits of his artistry.

Other portraits of this period are that of the Child Cistúe, dated 1790; of the Marchioness of Solana (p. 27), with his restrained use of gray tones only lightened by a few touches of color; the portrait of the actress La Tirana (p. 28), also in gray tones, and that of the art collector Sebastián Martínez, in blue tones (1792). During this period he created such tapestry designs as "The Straw Doll" (p. 26), "Children Climbing Tree," and "Boy Riding Ram."

After he had taken part in a meeting of the Academy on September 2, 1792, Goya went to Andalusia, where he fell very ill. He recovered, but for the rest of his life he was stone deaf—like Beethoven, with whom he had so much in common. His life changed completely, for his deafness separated him from people, forced him to withdraw into himself and to depend upon his powers of imagination and his memories. The *joie de vivre* of his earlier years gave way to melancholy and pessimism. A new period began for him as an artist: he now expressed in his work his innermost thoughts about people and the world.

At the end of 1793 Goya was able to resume his creative work. Some of his portraits from this and the following year, such as that of General Ricardos, show no loss of mastery. Of far greater importance, however, are the innovations contained in the paintings which Goya sent to Don Bernardo de Iriarte in January, 1794. In a letter accompanying them he called them "several cabinet pieces in which I have succeeded in retaining observations which are not permitted in normal commissions, as mere fantasy and additions resulting from whims may not be developed in such works."

For a long time it was supposed that Goya was referring to pictures which today hang in the Royal Academy of San Fernando, but the style of these pictures would seem to point to a later period. Their coloring and the heavy brush treatment are more like the works which were painted after May 2, 1808. So we may not say with certainty exactly which pictures

11

he sent to Iriarte, but his letter appears to provide sufficient proof of the increasing prominence which Goya began to give to fantasy.

Sánchez Cantón has established that the painter's connections with the Ducal House of Alba began at this time. In 1795 Goya mentioned in a letter that the Duchess of Alba had come to his studio "so that he might apply make-up to her face." The portrait of the Duke dates from the same year, and that of the Duchess, which is still hanging in the House of Alba, must have been painted immediately thereafter. The allusions to the young, pretty, and lighthearted Duchess which may be found in older works on Goya have hardly any basis in fact. She *was* young—practically still a child at her wedding—and she *was* a beauty, but she was not happy in her marriage. The Duke was much older than she was, and a sick man; he was a lover of music, widely different from her in temperament and interests. On June 9, 1796, he died, and the Duchess retired to Sanlúcar, in Andalusia, where Goya visited her. There, in 1797, he painted her portrait, which he kept for himself. In it the Duchess is dressed entirely in black and wears a mantilla; she also wears two rings, one inscribed "Alba" and one "Goya," but on the floor at her feet are the words "Only Goya," to which she points (p. 22).

While in Andalusia Goya completed two albums of drawings. They served later as the basis of various of his etchings in the "Caprichos" (Fancies) collection (1797-99). The Duchess of Alba appears in some of these, and in each the artist accuses her of fickleness. The beautiful etching "Volaverunt" (They Have Flown) is well known, but the most revealing is the unpublished "Dream of Falsehood and Fickleness," an indictment and an expression of his pain—a reproach which came from the depths of his heart and which he dared not publish.

Many have believed that the Duchess was the model for his

12

Maja paintings, but this would seem to be highly improbable, as these pictures would appear from their technique to have been done at a different period.

During these years several important events took place in Goya's life, including his appointment in September, 1795, to the post of Director of the Painting Department of the Academy after the death of the previous Director, his brother-in-law Francisco Bayeu. Only a short time before—in August—he had exhibited the beautiful pearl-gray portrait of his brother-in-law (p. 25), which resembles in tone other pictures from the same period, notably "The Naked Maja" (p. 55). Goya retained the post of director only for a short period; in April, 1797, owing to poor health, he submitted his resignation.

In the middle of 1798 he received a second important commission from the Duchess of Osuna for the Alameda. This time she ordered six pictures with witch motifs. Small cabinet pieces evolved from it, some of which depicted witch scenes and others well-known comedy scenes.

During the same year he was entrusted with decorating the Chapel of San Antonio de la Florida, in Madrid. Goya's frescoes in the dome of the Chapel depict people watching St. Anthony as he performs the miracle of bringing a dead man back to life (pp. 29, 30). Goya also decorated the trumpet arch of the main chapel with a triangle showing the Trinity surrounded by praying angels and angel groups pulling the gigantic red curtains halfway up. The execution of this picture shows an astonishing daring. Lafuente has already pointed out that Goya was far in advance of his time and that parts of these frescoes have characteristics similar to the techniques of Manet and Daumier.

In January, 1799, Goya signed a confirmation of a receipt from the Duchess of Osuna for four copies of his "Caprichos," which in the first edition comprised eighty prints.

13

With painstaking care and excellent technique—a combination of etching, aquatint, and even cold-needle etching—he created a series of prints to which very few may be compared in the history of the graphic arts.

Many of these etchings are based on his albums of Sanlúcar and Madrid. The first album differs from the second both in the subjects and in the drawing technique: it recaptures the carefree time which the artist spent in the company of the Duchess of Alba and her friends. The second presents scenes of daily life. In the closing pages we encounter something entirely new and different: graphic satire of the society of the time. Goya at this period was clearly under the influence of the rationalistic trend of thought of his friends and his reading.

It is in this context that we must understand the prints of the "Caprichos" collection. The etchings are, as the advertisement in the *Madrid Daily News* announced, a critical analysis of errors and vices. They do not appear to be personal attacks, as was for some time believed; we find, among other things, allusions to the fields of literature and the theater and a number of witch and goblin pictures. These illustrate the theme that "The Sleep of Reason Produces Monsters," the title of one of the most famous of these scenes (p. 41).

According to a letter that Goya wrote to his friend Ferrer many years later, in 1825, the collection was available for purchase for two days, during which period twenty-seven copies were sold. He also reported that he was denounced before the Inquisition, but apparently the matter did not come to a hearing, as Goya was allowed to retain the unsold copies. In 1803 he surrendered them to the King, together with the original printing plates. As compensation he received an annual pension of twelve thousand reals for his son, Francisco Xavier. When one takes into consideration the fact that the copies had been sold for 320 reals, this would not appear to have been a bad transaction for the artist. Furthermore, as this collection of the "Caprichos" were the first work of Goya's to become known outside of Spain, they made him an important figure and enabled him to exert an influence upon the entire European romantic school.

In the same year (1799) he painted several other important pictures, among which, for the Cathedral of Toledo, was "The Arrest of Christ," the rich and somber coloring of which reminds one of Rembrandt. Also at this time Goya painted the portrait of his friend, the writer Leandro Fernández de Moratín, and towards the end of the year, portraits of Queen María Luisa, first wearing a mantilla and then on horseback (p. 35) and an equestrian portrait of King Charles IV.

The Court was pleased with these portraits, and in October, 1799, Goya was appointed First Court Painter, with a good salary and additional expenses for maintenance of a carriage. He now stood at the peak of his artistic career, and his pictures of this period reflect his contentment and security.

In the spring of 1800 he received a commission for two works which became famous immediately after their execution. One is the portrait of the Countess of Chinchón, the most tender and delicate of all his portraits of women. The fair-haired young countess, Doña María Teresa de Bourbón, was married to the all-powerful minister Godoy (the lover of the Queen). In Goya's portrait the Countess is depicted as pregnant, and sits in a comfortable armchair, wearing a full white dress. Everything is white and hazy, and the dominant impression is one of youthful and pathetic frailty. Goya doubtless had a tender feeling for her, for he had known her as a little girl when he painted her parents in Arenas de San Pedro.

The other great work is the portrait of the family of Charles IV (p. 31). From the Queen's letters we learn that Goya finished the model studies in June, after which he intended to paint the group picture on the large canvas. He constructed it in the form of a frieze, which is formed by the row of members of the royal family before a wall lined with dark paintings. The central figure is the Queen, with the two youngest children (p. 33) at her side. To the left of the central group there is a second, dominated by Crown Prince Don Ferdinand, subsequently King Ferdinand VII; behind him is his brother Don Carlos and a female figure who turns her face away from the viewer and is presumably the future spouse—still anonymous—of the heir to the throne. Almost in semidarkness one can see the infant Doña María Josefa and further in the background, near the left picture frame, a self-portrait of the artist himself at work on a large canvas.

This painting inevitably reminds one of Velázquez's "Las Meninas" (The Noble Maidens), though it has not the same compactness. It differs completely from the family portraits of the court painters of the baroque period, for example that of the family of Philip V by Van Loo, which also hangs in the Prado, or even that of Charles IV and his family by the contemporary Spanish painter Vicente López. These pictures are full of pomp and courtly flattery. In Goya's painting, by comparison, though the royal family is posing in court dress and jewels, they stand in a relaxed manner before a simple palace wall. Movement is suggested solely through the balanced construction of the groups depicted, but one sees neither massive curtains nor regal and graceful gestures on the part of the subjects.

It is noteworthy that the heads in the sketches appear without any trace of the idealism which Goya gave them on the large canvas (p. 36). Although the portraits of the King and the Queen are not very flattering to them, it is possible that the royal subjects were actually uglier than Goya painted them.

It is a magnificent picture. Masterly alone is the amazingly realistic manner in which the painter reproduced the sheen of the materials and the glitter of medals. Equally remarkable is the relaxed and lifelike appearance of the figures. Without doubt "The Family of Charles IV" is a masterpiece of the painter's art for all time.

In 1808 Goya was sixty-two, an old man by the standards of that day. In that year there began for Spain a tragic period of war and revolution, initiated by the uprising at Aranjuez on March 18 and 19, which resulted in the abdication of Charles IV, the proclamation of his son as Ferdinand VII, and the imprisonment of Godoy. Shortly afterwards, on May 2, Madrid revolted against the Napoleonic troops who were entering Spain as "friends." Enticed by Napoleon, the Spanish royal family went to France, virtually as prisoners. On July 20 Joseph I, who had been proclaimed King of Spain by his brother, Napoleon, entered Madrid. A few days previously the French had been defeated in Andalusia. Joseph I left Madrid again on July 31, and on August 24 Ferdinand VII, still a captive in France, was once again proclaimed King in Madrid.

Now the whole of Spain rose against the invading armies, and English troop contingents hastened to the aid of the Spanish patriots. Napoleon went at the head of his army to Spain and rapidly advanced as far as Madrid. He soon withdrew in order to fight on other fronts. The fortunes of war fluctuated. The Spanish resistance at the two sieges of Saragossa and of Gerona became historic. Despite occasional victories the French were defeated, and in 1814 Ferdinand returned to Spain, wildly acclaimed by his people.

It is assumed that Goya spent part of these years in Madrid, but between the two sieges he would appear to have been in Saragossa and even to have spent some time in the field. Perhaps he was also with the Court of Joseph I in Valencia when it moved to the East Coast. It is not easy to ascertain his political position. On the one hand, he continued to live under the government of Joseph I as Court Painter, received honors, swore the requisite oaths of allegiance, and took part in public ceremonies and festivals. He also painted portraits of well-known French sympathizers, selected pictures from the Royal Collection for the Napoleonic Museum, and agreed to paint an allegorical portrait of Joseph I for the Madrid City Hall. On the other hand, he went to Saragossa, summoned by General Palafo, the defender of that city against the French. In the Academy he exhibited a portrait of the Duke of Wellington and described himself as "First Painter to the King" (Ferdinand VII).

This deviousness in behavior brought Goya, at the age of sixty-two, to a serious mental crisis. Together with some friends who sympathized with the French, he shared the opinion that Spain had not been all that it should have been, and for that reason he attacked the existing social system by the use of criticism and satire. With his friends, he believed in the principles of the revolutionary French philosophers. But at the same time he was outraged by the brutality of the French invaders. And he detested the subjection of Spain to a new dynasty forced upon the country by Napoleon.

It was from this mental state that there originated "Los Desastres de la Guerra" (The Disasters of War), a series of eighty drawings and etchings, to which must be added two further prints which were not included in the Academy editions but may be considered as the finishing touch to the Collection. This is an indictment of the French invaders and their treatment of the heroic Spanish patriots.

Many of the first prints in the series touch on this theme. Others deal with indirect consequences, such as scenes of hunger. The collection closes with seventeen prints which were given the title "Caprichos Enfáticos" by the Academy. In these Goya's

18

(Continued on page 73)

21

23

29

31

34

El sueño de la razon produce monstruos

43

44

45

47

48

50

56

58

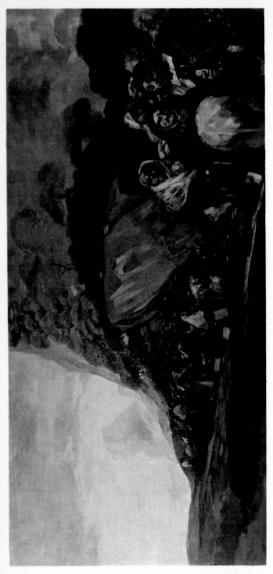

bitterness, his hatred of certain prominent personalities, his love of truth and freedom, and his hope for a peaceful future are all expressed.

The Spanish war for freedom against Napoleon was conducted more by individuals and small groups of resistance fighters, in sporadic attacks and acts of vengeance, than by battling armies. It was the people themselves who rose against the invaders and inflicted on them a decisive defeat. Goya recorded this struggle in his works of the period. His etchings portray vivid incidents of the war, such as individual moments of great heroism and tragedy, which he had seen himself or which he had learned of from eyewitnesses. These scenes in their terrifying beauty have more than a merely documentary character and have attained a permanent place in the history of art.

Goya produced several paintings of war scenes during the French occupation—for example, the small pictures which he kept in his own home and listed, in the Inventory of 1812, under the title "Disasters of War," and two large paintings which depict occurrences in Madrid on May 2 and 3, 1808. These are scenes from the battle of the practically unarmed people of Madrid against the mamelukes (mercenary troops composed of former slaves) on the Puerta del Sol (p. 60) and of the reprisals taken by the French, the shootings during the subsequent night (pp. 61, 63). In these paintings a new stage of Goya's artistry is reached—indeed, a new stage in art in general. There is nothing comparable to be found among earlier works, neither in respect of composition, in which so much intuitive genius has been invested, nor in the painting technique. The shapes are more suggested than carefully delineated, and the coloring vibrates with vitality. The bright colors—white shirt and yellowish trousers—of the central figure against a background of somber tones show a most effective use of dramatic lighting. By emphasizing certain details the painter achieves a powerful expression of emotion. The picture communicates an atmosphere of frenzy which both shocks and attracts the viewer.

During the years of the war and those following, Goya painted several important portraits. He produced the equestrian portraits of King Ferdinand VII, the less attractive portrait of the Duke of Wellington, and the somewhat similar but far more beautiful portrait of General Castaños, the Defender of Saragossa. He also painted a brilliantly colored bust portrait of Wellington, depicting his aquiline features as full of power and intelligence (p. 57), the portraits of some officers, and the unforgettable portrait of the Canon Juan Antonio Llorente, the historian of the Inquisition (p. 56), in black against a dark-gray background, with the red sash of the Order of Joseph as the sole touch of color.

At this point mention should be made of the very beautiful pictures from the Royal Academy of San Fernando, in Madrid. For a long time it was believed that these originated in the year 1794, when Goya had just recovered from his illness. His comments contained in his accompanying letter to the 1794 works are quoted on page 11. Today it is believed that these Academy pictures, to which the "Carnival Scene" (p. 70) belongs, are part of a series of paintings which were created during the war years. The heavy and yet sensitive brush strokes, the coloring, the "expressionism," and even the themes of several of the pictures show that they came later. Several genre pictures of this period have the central theme of labor: "The Water Carrier," "The Knife Grinder," and the life-size painting "The Blacksmith." Goya employed similar themes in pictures during his youth and also in several tapestry designs, but their presentation is now less idyllic. The workers no longer appear to be living a hard but nevertheless contented life; they are now pictured as doing an exhausting day's work. Goya was the first painter to express a point of view which became increasingly common during the nineteenth century.

To turn again to historic events: when Ferdinand VII returned, on May 7, 1814, to Madrid, a draft constitution was submitted by the representatives of the country gathered in the Cortes of Cadiz; it was completely ignored by the King, who fondly believed that he could always rely upon the tumultuous expression of loyalty which had greeted him on his return. Despite the fact that at that time he had been acclaimed as "The Desired One," Ferdinand VII was one of the worst kings in the records of history. As we shall see, this situation was not without influence upon the life of Goya and even upon his art.

Goya acknowledged Ferdinand VII and, together with the other members of the Academy, received him at the sitting of July 8, 1814. After his previous office of Painter to the Court had been given back to him, he created several official portraits of the monarch (p. 65), all based on the one study which he had used previously for the equestrian portraits. The changes in the King's features during the intervening six years were only suggested by Goya through more pronounced outlines. After the first two years of the return of Ferdinand to the throne, Goya never painted the monarch again.

The years from 1815 until Goya's departure for France produced a wonderful series of portraits, among them the elegant canvas of the Duke of San Carlos, painted for the Board of the Imperial Canal of Aragon, that of the Bishop of Marcópolis, the pictures of several ministers, and that of the Secretary of the Academy, José Luis de Munárriz. The Secretary was presumably instrumental in obtaining the commission for one of Goya's largest works, an enormous picture which now hangs in the Castres Museum. In all probability it depicts a sitting of the Royal Philippine Company, which maintained a branch office in Madrid from 1785 (p. 68). One sees a large chamber, unevenly lighted by a window on the right-hand side; in the semidarkness many people fill the benches on both sides. In the background the Board of the Company are seated on a stage, and in the center, somewhat higher than the gentlemen surrounding him, is the monarch. The uneven illumination gives the illusion of depth to the picture. The black and gray tones are lightened only by a few patches of color, mainly in the tapestry design. In his construction Goya appears to have competed with the painting "The Pure Maiden" by Velázquez, which also depicts a chamber dimly and unevenly lighted. This was the last picture that Goya produced as an official commission.

At the re-established Bourbon courts he continued to portray representatives of the families who had earlier engaged his services: one was of the House of Osuna—Doña Manuela Téllez-Girón (1816), in classical garments of light color, and her brother, the tenth Count of Osuna, with horse and lackeys, in front of a landscape background. This last picture is reminiscent of Reynolds. But the trend of fashion and taste now moved in new directions, and the painter who was now in great demand at court was Vicente López.

Goya did not stand still, however. In 1816, at the age of seventy, he announced a new series of thirty-three etchings: "Tauromaquia" (The Art of Bullfighting). The first etchings illustrate the *Historical Letter on the Origin and Development of Bullfighting* by Nicolás Fernández de Moratín, but after completing twelve pages Goya dropped this idea and proceeded to work from his own memories of bullfights, and in the last etchings fantasy played a big part. Goya was a great master of the aquatint technique. He would leave some areas on the plate untouched, in order to strengthen the light effect, or he would cover them with a mere wash of color in order to accentuate the dramatic tension. He simplified the scenes by depicting only a few people, drawn with the accuracy of the connoisseur of the bullfight.

In the following years Goya devoted more time to religious paintings. Besides "The Ascension of Mary" (1812), of little importance, he painted, in 1817, "Saints Justa and Rufina" for the Chapel of Seville, and in 1819 "The Last Communion of St. José de Calasanz" for the Piarist Church in Madrid and the almost monochrome expressive "Christ on the Mount of Olives."

He also did portraits of his friends the architect Juan Antonio Cuervo (1819) and Tiburcio Pérez (1820), as well as of his physician, Doctor Arrieta. In this picture Goya shows himself taking medicine from the hands of the Doctor; a prominent dedication on this picture states that Arrieta had saved his life during his "bad and dangerous illness."

It is probable that the series of etchings entitled "Proverbios" (Proverbs) or "Disparates" (Absurdities) were created during the period of convalescence following this illness. The collected volume at the Academy contains eighteen prints, but there are four others in existence of which earlier impressions are known to have been made. The fantastic nature of the subjects of these etchings defies any attempt at interpretation. It has been generally believed that the pictures were based on Spanish proverbs. With absolute mastery of the techniques of etching, Goya created strange and portentous figures. On the basis of their dark tone and gloomy fantasy, these etchings would appear to have originated in the same world of imagination as that of the paintings with which Goya decorated two rooms of his villa on the Manzanares River. He had purchased the residence in 1819 and continued to work there until 1824, when he left for France.

The fact that the number of well-known pictures of this period is so small is no doubt explained by the strenuous nature of the tasks which this 76-year-old man had undertaken in decorating his house and in completing the "Disparates" series.

The so-called "black paintings" from his house hang today in the Prado Museum in Madrid. They are almost monochromes. While here and there a red or blue dab of color lightens the monotony, and a touch of gold gives a highlight, brown, gray, and black tones dominate the pictures. In these paintings, which were only intended for himself, Goya gave his imagination free rein. In some there are intimations of personal matters which are difficult for us to understand. In the majority Goya pictured his world in symbols; he painted to please himself and projected his own dreams and visions, so that the basest realities were interwoven with the progeny of his imagination.

Ferdinand VII had refused to acknowledge the constitution drafted by the Cortes in 1814. In 1820, however, he was obliged to do so by a military revolt led by General Riego—an event which must have filled Goya with satisfaction. He participated in the meeting of the Academy on the occasion of the adoption of the new constitution. The ideas expressed in his drawings and etchings leave no doubt whatsoever as to his democratic convictions.

The liberal regime did not last very long. In May, 1823, the Duke of Angoulême, at the head of a French army, invaded Spain with the object of restoring the absolute monarchy. The liberals lost, and Ferdinand reigned once more as undisputed monarch. Fearing persecution, Goya, on September 17, presented his grandchild Mariano with the villa on the Manzanares and took refuge with friends.

On May 2, 1824, Goya requested the King's permission to take a six-month convalescent cure at Plombières in France, which was granted. The route which Goya took, however, shows that this was a mere excuse; for he did not journey to Plombières in the North, but to Bordeaux in the South of France. He arrived there at the end of June and immediately left for Paris, possibly to visit the portrait exhibition which had just opened there. It is more likely, however, that this journey was mainly directed towards settling financial matters.

Back in Bordeaux, Goya fell ill, but he continued to paint and to produce lithographs. Since his first lithograph, "The Old Spinner" (p. 43), was dated 1819, it may be presumed that he had worked from that time in this medium, which was new in those days. Among his many lithographs the four greatest are generally considered to be the "Bulls of Bordeaux," which epitomize the experience of a lifetime. In these highly evocative scenes the bullfight is reduced to the simplest terms. The figures of the toreadors are shown in bold strokes and those of the massive but agile bulls are vigorously portrayed. Dominant in these pictures is the contrast of vivid highlights against heavy shadows. Mathéron has recorded how Goya worked. He placed the stone plate on his easel as though it were a canvas and, when working, would approach it closely and then step back to see if the desired effect had been achieved.

Despite his age Goya returned once again to Madrid to obtain an extension of his foreign-residence permit, so that he might live in France on the pension which was granted to him in 1825. While he was in Madrid, Vicente López painted a portrait of him in which he appears still healthy and strong. In July, 1825, we find him back in Bordeaux with the artist Rosario Weiss and her family. Among the friends around him was the writer Nicolás Fernández de Moratín, whose correspondence has left us a wealth of anecdotes. In 1826 Goya painted a French friend, Santiago Galós, and a little later Don Juan Muguiro (p. 64) upon whose portrait he proudly inscribed "at the age of 80 years in Bordeaux, May 1827." In this portrait of soft coloring, Muguiro sits in a dark-blue coat before a greenish background, from which the mighty figure and the lighter patches of face,

79

shirt front, hands, and the paper which they are holding, stand out distinctly. This picture lives through the powerful presence of the subject: a contented, substantial citizen. Both subject and treatment suggest Manet.

Goya painted other pictures of some friends and of his grandchild Mariano, and what is thought to be his last portrait, that of José Pío de Molina. His last female portrait is the "Milkmaid of Bordeaux" (p. 72), which is painted with short, crossed brush strokes.

Goya was being visited by his grandchild and was awaiting a visit from his son when, after a new attack of illness, he died on the night of April 15-16, 1828. Right up to his last day he was full of the will to live, and full of creative energy and imagination. One of his own drawings may be considered a spiritual self-portrait; it shows an aged man painfully advancing with the aid of two sticks; the caption is "I am still learning" (p. 58).

— — —

Any attempt to sum up Goya's extensive and varied artistic works in a few words is impossible. But at the end of our brief presentation of Goya as man and artist, let us sum up his main stages of development.

He soon mastered the conventional style of expression of that time and from the copying of the Neapolitan painters he went on to acquire the style of the Santa Barbara school. Soon he achieved an entirely personal style, in which he expressed his *joie de vivre* and, subsequently, a wide range of spiritual experiences. Together with this development, a continuous pattern of change took place on his always varied palette; from dark, glowing tones to the multicolor of the rococo, then to gray, and later to an even greater variety of contrast, culminating with somber shades.

His etchings based on Velázquez gave him a deep understanding of that painter's works. He then turned to the art of one-color presentation, whose variety of nuances he, among so very few, was able to utilize. Simultaneously with the etchings he discovered even more possibilities of expression. The satirical, critical, humorous Goya awoke, doubtless under the influence of a literary current, but also because of the complete change in the pattern of his life occasioned by his deafness. Convalescence from an illness appears always to have heralded the inception of a new series of etchings.

These series reveal the personality of Goya from many different sides—as critic of society, as patriot, as reformer, as enemy of the French despite his humanitarian and liberal ideas, as lover of bullfights, and as a person who was capable of giving striking form to his fantasies and nightmares.

While landscape remained a closed book to him, and he had no understanding of animals, these deficiencies do not count when compared with his clear vision of the human personality. Men and women appear in his portraits exactly as they were, and as his perceptive eye saw them. Formal perfection and beauty according to rule he soon put aside. To portray his models, he did not need much color, nor had he need of perfection of contour—though as a graphic artist and engraver he was capable of executing this superbly. He was satisfied with evocative dabs of color and lines filled with vibrating strength. This development towards economy of medium and expression is reminiscent of Beethoven, and it brought his art to a zenith of great humanity.

LIST OF ILLUSTRATIONS

44 THE WOMEN GIVE COURAGE
   (Los Desastres de la Guerra, No. 4)
   1808-15; etching

45 THE WAY IS HARD (Los Desastres de la Guerra, No. 14)
   1808-15; etching

46 CARTLOADS FOR THE CEMETERY
   (Los Desastres de la Guerra, No. 64)
   1808-15; etching

47 THIS IS THE TRUTH (Los Desastres de la Guerra, No. 82)
   1808-15; drawing in red chalk for etching

48 AGILITY AND DARING OF JUANITO APIÑANI IN THE MADRID
   ARENA (Tauromaquia, No. 20)
   About 1815; etching

49 THE SAD DEATH OF PEPE ILLO IN THE MADRID ARENA
   (Tauromaquia, No. 33)
   About 1815; etching

50 THE DANCING GIANT (Los Proverbios, No. 4)
   Before 1820; etching

51 THE CASTANET DANCERS (Los Proverbios, No. 12)
   Before 1820; etching

52 FLYING MEN (Los Proverbios, No. 13)
   Before 1820; etching

53 THE PROCESSION OF THE FLAGELLANTS ON GOOD FRIDAY
   1812-15; oil; 16×28½ in.; Academia de San Fernando,
   Madrid

54 THEY TAKE ADVANTAGE OF THE SITUATION
   (Los Desastres de la Guerra, No. 16)
   1808-15; red-crayon study for etching; 5×8 in.; Prado,
   Madrid